BANNOCK REPUBLIC

BANNOCK REPUBLIC

KENNETH T. WILLIAMS

Bannock Republic
first published 2011 by
Scirocco Drama
An imprint of J. Gordon Shillingford Publishing Inc.

Scirocco Drama Editor: Glenda MacFarlane
Cover design by Terry Gallagher/Doowah Design Inc.
Author photo by Stefen Winchester
Production photos by peter j. christensen
Printed and bound in Canada on 100% post-consumer recycled paper.

We acknowledge the financial support of the Manitoba Arts Council and The Canada Council for the Arts for our publishing program.

Production inquiries should be addressed to:
Charles Northcote
140 Wolfrey Avenue
Toronto, ON M4K 1L3
416-466-4929

Library and Archives Canada Cataloguing in Publication

Williams, Kenneth T., 1965-
Bannock Republic / Kenneth T. Williams.

A play.
ISBN 978-1-897289-63-1

I. Title.

PS8645.I4525B35 2011 C812'.6 C2011-901114-X

J. Gordon Shillingford Publishing
P.O. Box 86, RPO Corydon Avenue, Winnipeg, MB Canada R3M 3S3

For my parents

Characters

ZIA MARKHAAVI:	She's the South African bureau chief for a major television cable news station. Her family fled Iran after the revolution and moved to Israel. She married Isaac 12 years ago. She's played by the same actor as Destiny.
DESTINY CHARLES:	Young, beautiful, intelligent, she owns her own forensic accounting firm and is the newly appointed third party manager for the Thunder Cree First Nation. She's also an exact double for Zia, Isaac's dead wife.
ISAAC THUNDERCHILD:	Late 40s, recently elected chief of the Thunder Cree First Nation. He's an internationally acclaimed photojournalist who hasn't picked up the cameras in nearly 10 years.
JACOB THUNDERCHILD:	Isaac's cousin, in his late 40s, sober for nearly a year, now a video-journalist for the Aboriginal Peoples Television Network.

Setting

Various war zones. Thunder Cree First Nation, a fictional reserve in central Saskatchewan.

Time

1996-1999, 2009

Production History

Bannock Republic was co-produced by Persephone Theatre and the Saskatchewan Native Theatre Company, February 4–21, 2010, with the following cast:

JACOB..........Mark Dieter

ISSAC..........Curtis Peeteetucer

ZIA / DESTINY..........Paula Jean Prudat

Directed by Herbie Barnes

Set and Props Design by Carla Orosz

Lighting Design by Bill McDermott

Costume Design by Evgenia Mikhaylova

Sound Design by Jody Longworth

Technician: Tanqueray Fisher

Stage Manager: Diana Domm

Kenneth T. Williams

Kenneth T. Williams is a Cree playwright, filmmaker, and journalist from the George Gordon First Nation in Saskatchewan. His plays *Gordon Winter*, *Café Daughter*, *Thunderstick* (Scirocco Drama, 2010), *Suicide Notes*, and *Three Little Birds* have been produced across Canada. As well as writing plays, Kenneth has edited three television series and teaches playwriting at the University of Saskatchewan. He is the first aboriginal writer to earn an M.F.A. in playwriting from the University of Alberta. He currently resides in Saskatoon

Act I

Scene 1

War Zone, 1996. ISAAC and ZIA scramble for cover. An explosion, a close one, makes them duck.

ZIA: Where did that come from?

ISAAC: Journalists! We're journalists, for chrissakes!

ZIA: I don't think they speak English.

ISAAC: *(French.)* Journalistes! *(Italian.)* Giornalistas!

More shooting close by.

ZIA: Maybe you should try German.

ISAAC: Journalisten— You're making fun of me, aren't you.

ZIA: I don't think these people care how we say "reporter." Keep your head down.

ISAAC: Can't get a shot without—

A shot ricochets nearby. ISAAC ducks.

ZIA: Without getting shot? Careful!

She checks him over.

ISAAC: I'm OK. I'm OK.

ZIA: Don't scare me like that.

ISAAC: Sorry. Any thoughts on dinner?

She looks through a small backpack.

ZIA: Italian?

She holds up a can of ravioli. It gets shot out of her hand.

ISAAC: We had Italian yesterday.

ZIA: Tex-Mex?

She holds up a can of chili. It gets shot out of her hand.

ISAAC: Gives me gas.

A nearby explosion.

ZIA: No one will notice, my dear.

ISAAC: That all we got?

ZIA: We have some rations the Canadians gave us. Not very appetizing. Freeze-dried spinach! Who freeze-dries spinach?

She pulls out an individual meal pack, IMP, from the backpack.

It's open.

She looks inside the box and pulls out smaller jewelery box.

Isaac? What's this?

ISAAC: Open it.

It's a diamond ring.

ZIA: Oh my god.

ISAAC: Zia Maarkhavi, it's been 4 years since we met and—

Machine gun fire makes them duck.

ZIA: Get to the fucking point!

ISAAC: Marry me.

ZIA: Yes!

She grabs him and kisses him.

Your timing needs work.

ISAAC: It's our anniversary. I don't care where we are.

ZIA: A diamond seems so European, so bourgeois.

ISAAC: I'll take it back.

ZIA: No, no. I'm not saying that. I'm just wondering how your people express engagement to marriage.

ISAAC: Hickies.

ZIA: What's a hickey?

ISAAC: Let me show you.

He starts passionately kissing her neck. She screams. The war fades. "Hava nagila" gets louder. They face the audience, as two newlyweds, shouts of "mazel tov!" then slow smoky jazz plays in the background. Holding each other, they dance slowly to the music.

ZIA: Happy anniversary.

ISAAC: Doesn't feel right. No one's shooting at us.

ZIA: You don't want us to fall into a rut, do you?

They dance some more.

Tell me you love me.

ISAAC: I love you.

ZIA: In Cree.

ISAAC: I can't.

ZIA: You can still learn.

ISAAC: Only if I went back home.

ZIA: What's stopping you?

Jazz fades into the Jewish song of mourning. A giant yellow Star of David with "Juden" scrawled on it. They are in Yed Veshim, the Holocaust memorial in Israel.

You know, I like my anniversary locations better.

ISAAC: It's the only day we could be here before we leave Israel.

ZIA: But why here? There's so much pain here. And anger.

ISAAC: At least they acknowledge it.

ZIA: Ken, ken, I know, I know. That's why my father brought us here when the Ayatollah came to power. He was afraid Jews would be dragged out of their homes and slaughtered in the streets. And it's all I heard about growing up here. "Never again! Never again!"

ISAAC: Would you rather it was suppressed? Wiped from the memory of history?

ZIA: I'd rather live in a world that didn't need memorials.

Sounds of a hospital. ZIA is lying on a bed.

ISAAC: Happy anniversary.

ZIA: Honestly, my love, you pick the worst places to celebrate our anniversary.

ISAAC: Next one's yours. I promise.

ZIA: If there's a next one.

ISAAC: Don't say that.

ZIA: Please, my dear, after all we've seen, you honestly believe in miracles? Our tragedy is so small. I'm not suffering. Much. We're luckier than most, my love.

ISAAC: I love you Zia Maarkhavi.

ZIA: Say it in Cree.

ISAAC: I can't.

ZIA: Go home. You have to go home, my love.

ZIA fades away. A cantor sings the Kaddish of mourning. ISAAC places a stone on her headstone. The music fades.

Black out.

Scene 2

In the darkness we hear two vehicles approaching from opposite directions, driving fast on a gravel road. Spot on JACOB Thunderchild. He's got an unlit cigarette in his lips. He tries to coordinate driving, reading a map, holding a cell phone and lighting his cigarette.

JACOB: Yes, I know it's against company policy to drive and talk on the phone but you called me and I know how paranoid you get when no one answers. *(Pause.)* Yes you do! *(Pause.)* You do!

He takes the cigarette out of his mouth.

I can smoke if I fucking want! It's my car! *(Pause.)* It's in the impound. No one told you? I'm surprised. *(Pause.)* I was NOT drinking! Christ, one crash and— OK OK, two crashes but the second one was— *(Pause.)* I'm on the way to Thunder Cree to cover their high school graduation. *(Pause.)* Why? Because you assigned it to me! *(Pause.)* You did, too. *(Pause.)* Yes, you did! You said it was "national news." How is getting Grade Twelve "national" news? I'm tired of these bullshit stories!

He looks at the map. Lights up on DESTINY who has a bluetooth-like earpiece and is talking to Rick on her Blackberry. She balances a naturopath-like cleansing drink and steering wheel in one hand.

DESTINY: Rick, it's Destiny. I just wanted to let you know that business is taking me to Montreal this weekend. Can I call you when I'm there? I'm staying at that bed and breakfast on Rue Rene Levesque. You remember the one, right? Just above Vieux Montreal?

Spotlight on JACOB.

JACOB: Good news story? We're covering the graduation of these fifteen kids but ignoring the hundred or so who dropped out. How the fuck is that a "good news" story?

Back to DESTINY.

DESTINY: I love saying that—Vieux Montreal. Is my French sounding better? If you have some time this weekend I think we should get together. Totally casual. No romantic dinners or quiet walks along the river. Just coffee. Nothing with any strings. I promise.

Back to JACOB.

JACOB: I want to do something significant. Something that has real impact.

Back to DESTINY.

DESTINY: I promise. OK? That sound OK? I'll call you when I get there.

Back to JACOB.

JACOB: Like the story I pitched at the last story meeting. *(Pause.)* Yes, I was serious!

DESTINY: I still think we can make this work.

Rick Astley's "Never Gonna Give You Up" plays on her radio. She gets transfixed.

Ooooooh Rick.

Lights on both.

DESTINY & JACOB: Fuck me!

Brakes screech. A collision. Lights up reveal two cars entangled. Dazed, they get out of their cars. DESTINY is still holding the drink, JACOB is still holding the map, a broken, unlit cigarette dangles from his lips. They look around.

DESTINY: Hey, buddy. Watch where you're going.

JACOB: Wasn't my fault. You just came out of nowhere.

DESTINY: Yeah, right. *(Her phone is dead.)* Does your phone work?

He looks at his car.

JACOB: Oooooh, Stella.

She searches her car again. Pulls out a naturopath-like cleansing drink.

DESTINY: How far is Thunder Cree from here? My GPS crapped out after I left North Battleford.

JACOB: Why are you going to Thunder Cree?

DESTINY: None of your business.

JACOB: You have relations there?

DESTINY: I just told you "it's none of your business" and you then you proceed to stick your nose in it. It was a simple question—one, any person with a tiny shred of human decency would have no problem answering "how far is Thunder Cree from here?" Is it because you lack basic empathy? Maybe you like watching people squirm because you have something that others need? The small power you have in your hands you need to lord over others! Is that the kind of person you are? Huh? A sociopath? Well?

Pause.

JACOB: I love you.

He pulls out an engagement ring from his pocket and offers it to her.

It's barely used. Only four previous owners.

DESTINY: The pawn tag is still on it.

He rips off the tag.

JACOB: Sorry. I was short of cash and Stella needed some new wheels. But it's a half-carat, near flawless, rosette in a platinum mount—

DESTINY: Who's Stella?

JACOB: My car.

He taps the roof.

DESTINY: You pawned this ring for that piece of shit?

JACOB: Hey! Have some respect.

DESTINY: It's just a car.

JACOB: Stella isn't just a car. She's a miracle. Mechanics said she was a lost cause because they could no longer find parts for her steering, suspension or brakes. They called her "an unfixable hunk of junk...a menace...death trap." But I never gave up on her. Because I believe if you love something unconditionally, it will thrive. It will do the impossible. Long after the engine light burnt out, she ran without a complaint. Six hundred thousand kilometers she ran. On love. Not gas, not oil, not tires, but love.

Pause.

I'm going to miss you, girl. There'll never be another like you. Thanks for the memories.

DESTINY: Be a man and put her out of her misery.

She mimics firing a rifle into Stella's engine.

JACOB: Mock me. I don't care. At least I have love.

ISAAC enters riding a mountain bike. He's totally fixated on DESTINY and crashes into the cars.

JACOB: Ike! Cousin! You alright?

ISAAC: Jacob? I thought I saw...[a ghost]...I'm OK.

DESTINY: You wouldn't happen to have a phone, would you?

ISAAC stares, still a little stunned from the crash.

Did the short bus forget to pick you up, buddy?

JACOB: He's not retarded. He's my cousin. Probably the smartest man you'll ever meet. He went to Oxford University. In England.

DESTINY: Really? Oxford?

JACOB: In England. Yes, really. *(To ISAAC.)* Tell her, Isaac.

ISAAC nods.

ISAAC: Shalom.

DESTINY & JACOB: Shalom?

DESTINY: You should wear a helmet when you ride.

ISAAC: No, sorry. I'm Isaac. Isaac Thunderchild. And you're right. I should wear a... What?...I didn't expect anyone down this road. Normally deserted.

DESTINY: Deserted? That's just great.

ISAAC: Since they twinned the highway. Sorry, you are?

DESTINY: Destiny Charles.

ISAAC: Destiny.

DESTINY: Do you have a phone?

ISAAC: Really? Destiny?

DESTINY: Oh my god. The idiots, they are gathering. Yes! It's really "Destiny!"

JACOB: He went to Oxford.

ISAAC: In England! *(Points to her car.)* Is that a hybrid?

DESTINY: Listen Oxford-boy, do you have a phone? You know, a magic-ringy-dingy-talkie machine?

ISAAC: You mean, like a cell phone?

DESTINY: I'm on a tight deadline and I don't have time for these games! You may be used to the slo-mo-anything goes pace but I have people who rely on me to do my job. I have to maintain a payroll.

ISAAC: OK, OK, calm down. My phone's back at my place.

DESTINY: So why don't you hop on your bikey and pedal back home and get your stupid phone and get me out of here.

JACOB: God, you're beautiful.

DESTINY: *(Indicating JACOB.)* And take him with you. Please.

JACOB: I can't help it. I've always loved strong women.

ISAAC picks up the bike. The frame is bent.

ISAAC: Won't get far on this.

DESTINY: God! Really!

She grabs another cleansing shake from her SUV, cracks it and slugs it all back at once.

What are you clowns looking at?

She belches and tosses the can.

JACOB: An angel.

ISAAC: Hey, hey, haven't you heard of recycling?

ISAAC picks up the can. He and JACOB read it.

JACOB: Is that Chinese?

DESTINY: It's a homeopathic cleansing shake made from Tibetan goji berries. It removes toxins and restores balance! Balance! Something your stupid chief and council don't seem to understand.

ISAAC: Hey! I'm the chief of Thunder Cree.

DESTINY: Sooooo. You're the one responsible for this mess.

ISAAC: What mess?

JACOB: You're the chief?

ISAAC: Six months. *(To DESTINY.)* What mess?

DESTINY: It's confidential. For you and the band council only.

JACOB: "Confidential" eh? This can't be good.

He suddenly remembers his camera in the trunk of his car. He starts assembling it in secret.

ISAAC: I don't recall any "confidential" meetings coming up. Who do you work for?

DESTINY: I have my own company.

ISAAC: And what does your company do?

DESTINY: We should talk in private. With the other band councilors. Not out here in front of—

JACOB has the camera assembled and is now taping them.

What do you think you're doing!

JACOB: What kind of mess are we talking about here?

ISAAC: Who do you work for?

DESTINY: *(To JACOB.)* Get out of here!

JACOB: Hey, I'm on your side. Got to keep these chiefs honest. *(To ISAAC.)* Is it a problem with the election? Too many dead voters again?

ISAAC: There was no problem with the election.

JACOB: I dunno, chief, "confidential" meetings are never a good thing.

ISAAC: "Chief?" Now it's chief?

JACOB: You're news now, Isaac. I can't play favourites because you're family.

ISAAC: Why don't you ask her what this is all about because I haven't got a clue.

JACOB points the camera at DESTINY. Pause.

JACOB: Marry me.

ISAAC: Oh geez. *(To DESTINY.)* So what's this about? You work for the feds?

DESTINY: This is better left for private—

ISAAC: Definitely feds.

DESTINY: I didn't say I work with the federal government.

ISAAC: It was the way you didn't say it that pretty much proved to me that you do.

DESTINY: I have my own company.

ISAAC: Selling Tibetan homeopathic cleansing tonics?

DESTINY: No!

ISAAC: This isn't hard to figure out. You're not with the AFN because you're alone. No big entourage that follows AFN people everywhere. And since we're not meeting at the nearest casino you're definitely not from the FSIN. So that leaves the feds or the province. You're not with the province because you haven't rescheduled our meeting three times and then cancelled it. That leaves the federal government. And only two departments bother with us—Health Canada and Indian Affairs. And Health Canada doesn't use mercenaries.

JACOB: Nice work, cousin.

ISAAC: And who are you working for now?

JACOB: APTN.

ISAAC: And you're doing a story on me because you knew she was coming?

JACOB: That's being a little paranoid. It's just a coincidence.

ISAAC: I don't like coincidences when you're around.

JACOB: Oh come on. We had fun the last time.

ISAAC: So much fun, I didn't see you for ten years. Why are you really here if it's not to cover…her arrival?

DESTINY: Destiny!

ISAAC: Destiny. Sorry. *(To JACOB.)* Jake, what are you doing here? What's the story?

JACOB turns off the camera. He sighs heavily.

JACOB: I'm actually ashamed to say this, us being professional journalists and everything.

ISAAC: Yes?

JACOB: I'm covering your Grade Twelve graduation.

ISAAC: Since when is a Grade Twelve graduation national news?

JACOB: I know, eh! It all started because one of our other reporters covered a Grade Twelve grad and then every fucking high school principal on a reserve figured "if they're news, then we're news" and we get flooded with press releases from all over the country announcing Grade Twelve, Grade Nine, Grade Six, kindergarten "graduations." Do you actually "graduate" from kindergarten? Do you put that on a resumé when you apply for a job?

ISAAC: So you do it because everyone else is doing it?

JACOB: There's nothing original about TV news, Ike. If I'm not reporting what everyone else is reporting, my boss doesn't think I'm doing my job.

ISAAC: Doesn't sound rewarding.

JACOB: I'm a serious journalist. I shouldn't be stuck doing this bullshit.

ISAAC: So you've come back to this reserve after twenty-five years to cover a graduation ceremony that happened last week.

JACOB: It was what?

ISAAC: How serious are you when you can't read a press release?

DESTINY laughs.

JACOB: I didn't "get" the press release. My assignment editor sent me here. Set me up, that bastard. God, it's bad enough I haven't filed a story in two weeks. Now this!

DESTINY: Hey, hey, hey! Shouldn't we be focusing on getting out of here or getting help?

ISAAC: Only two options—wait or walk. But almost no one uses this road anymore. Except to go to the bison ranch.

DESTINY: You have a bison ranch?

JACOB: How far of a walk?

ISAAC: To the reserve? Two hours. Maybe three for you.

JACOB: Walking?

DESTINY: How far is the ranch from here? We could walk there and call for help.

JACOB: Why are we so focused on walking?

ISAAC: We can't call for help. We have the ranch but no bison. No bison, no staff, so we don't have a phone line or anything there.

DESTINY: No bison? Someone leave the gate open and they all run away. Typical reserve management.

ISAAC: Hey, it wasn't our fault. We had everything ready

to go. We used our land claim money to buy the land. We had local ranchers willing to donate their time to help our young people learn the business. We negotiated a great deal with a meat processing plant. We had our business model approved by the feds and the province. Everything was going perfectly. We were about to ship our first herd when some no-name bureaucrat within the department of Indian Affairs decided that we needed another approval for the expense. And it just cascaded from there! The seller found another buyer, so we lost that herd.

DESTINY: Well you should've got the approval.

ISAAC: We had the approval! There was no reason to question the expense. After Indian Affairs realized it was their mistake they released the funds but it was too late. Do you know how hard it is to find a bison herd? Or the money it costs to make sure they're not carrying any diseases that will affect local cattle? Millions of bucks lost because of a bureaucrat. Not to mention the fifty jobs it would've created. And it wasn't just us. The meat processor lost out and so did some of the ranchers around here who wanted to lease their land for pasture. They were so pissed they sent the member of parliament to "go give Indian Affairs heck!" Poor bastard didn't know what he was up against.

JACOB: You just let a white man walk into Indian Affairs? Without help! How could you, Isaac?

ISAAC: If I knew what he was up to, I would've stopped him.

DESTINY: Oh you guys are full of crap.

JACOB: Hey, taking on Indian Affairs isn't for amateurs. You'll never find a more wretched hive of scum and villainy.

DESTINY: That's from Star Wars, you idiot.

JACOB: Well, it's definitely the Dark Side, if you know what I mean.

ISAAC: I don't know what INAC did to this guy but he starts shaking and twitching when you ask him about it.

JACOB: Poor bastard. So what are you going to do with the land?

ISAAC: Not much we can do with it. BSE wiped out the ranchers here so we can't even lease it as pasture. And no one's in a buying mood, so selling is not an option. We're stuck with it, raising wild grass and gophers. I'm willing to consider most options now.

DESTINY: It won't be your problem much longer. I might as well tell you now, since we're going to be stuck together for the next few hours, but Indian Affairs has appointed me your third party manager.

ISAAC: What!

JACOB: Way to go, cuz. Six months as chief and you're already in third party. *(A lá Darth Vader.)* Isaac, I am your third party manager.

ISAAC: Shut up, Jake!

DESTINY: That's why I was coming to see you. And the band council. Today. Decision was made last week.

She hands him a letter.

That's from the minister himself.

ISAAC quickly reads the letter.

ISAAC: Wait a minute. There's a process. INAC is supposed to negotiate this with us.

DESTINY: They did. With Chief Charlie.

ISAAC: He's the last chief.

DESTINY: I'm guessing he failed to inform you.

ISAAC: It doesn't matter if he informed me or not. I'm the new chief. We should be starting at square one. I have plans for getting this band out of this mess.

DESTINY: And I'll gladly take them under consideration.

ISAAC: You don't have the right to do this.

DESTINY: I not only have the right, chief, but I have the responsibility. To your people on this reserve and to the taxpayers of this country. For too long, conditions on our reserves have gone from bad to intolerable because of thieving or incompetent chiefs. Riding around in their big trucks. If they had any real balls they'd be fighting for their people instead of making sure they have more and everyone else has less. They keep us hungry. They hoard for themselves. Then intimidate us if we try to speak up. And government after government has done nothing about it. But there's a new sheriff town, bub. This federal government takes accountability and transparency very seriously.

ISAAC: So how much is my band paying you?

DESTINY: That is none of your business.

ISAAC: Transparency, huh?

DESTINY: Daylight's burning, chief. We should get going.

JACOB: Hey, hey! We shouldn't leave the scene of an accident.

ISAAC: You can stay here if you want. I'll try get a ride when we get to the rez.

JACOB sighs and starts getting his gear from

Stella—which includes a big suitcase, a large camera case, a tripod, and about eight half-filled twenty-sixers of booze.

ISAAC: You still on the sauce.

JACOB: No. These are just for emergencies. *(Beat.)* In case Stella ran out of gas!

ISAAC: Even your car runs on booze!

DESTINY: She's dead. Just dump them.

She moves to take them. He holds them to his chest.

JACOB: No no no no no no.

DESTINY: We haven't got time for this nonsense.

JACOB: Move on ahead. I'll catch up.

ISAAC: Anything I can help you with?

JACOB: No, I'm responsible for it. I'll carry it.

He pours the half-empty bottles into each other to reduce the number he's carrying.

DESTINY: That's disgusting.

ISAAC: You don't know the half of it. *(To JACOB.)* This way, remember?

JACOB: I remember, I remember. Go. I'll catch up.

ISAAC and DESTINY exit. JACOB keeps filling the bottles. He waits till they're gone. He stares at the liquor and then at Stella, and thinks about it.

Fuck!

He tries pouring it out but can't.

Fuck fuck fuck fuck fuck fuck fuck!

He accidentally kicks Stella.

Oh shit! Sorry baby.

He kisses Stella. He gathers the bottles into the bags, grabs his stuff, balances them and hurries off in the direction of ISAAC and DESTINY.

Black out.

Scene 3

They enter carrying their luggage, ISAAC is carrying most of JACOB's stuff. JACOB is winded.

JACOB: OK, OK. Smoke break.

DESTINY: Not again.

JACOB: I like to pace myself.

ISAAC: It's going to take us a couple more hours…at this pace.

DESTINY: Come on.

JACOB: Hang on.

He searches himself for a smoke.

DESTINY: I say we leave him.

He lights up and inhales deeply.

You don't look so good.

JACOB: Me? I'm in the best shape of my life. *(Coughs.)*

DESTINY: You call this "in shape?"

JACOB: Round is a shape. And I didn't say "in shape." I said, "best shape." I'm doing yoga and everything.

He does some beginner yoga poses with the burning cigarette dangling from his lips.

Ta da!

He coughs, then passes out.

DESTINY: Oh great.

ISAAC: Hey cousin…cuz…lard ass! Get up, you're not fooling anyone.

ISAAC kicks him.

DESTINY: Tell him we haven't got time for this.

ISAAC: Jake!

Kicks him harder.

DESTINY: Stop fucking around, Jacob!

ISAAC: Jake?

Realizes something's wrong and quickly checks him out.

Shit, he's not breathing. No pulse, either.

DESTINY: Really? This is really happening!

She pushes him aside and starts CPR.

Go get help! *(Pause.)* Go!

ISAAC exits, running. she continues CPR. Rhythmic to CPR compressions.

Come on, come on. I have to be in Montreal.

She slaps JACOB's chest. He coughs and gasps and groans. He tries to sit up.

Relax, relax.

JACOB: Good idea.

He lies back down. He notices the still burning cigarette and takes a long inhale.

DESTINY: How do you feel?

JACOB: Never…been…better. What happened?!

DESTINY: You were doing yoga then had a heart attack.

JACOB: I didn't know yoga was so dangerous. They should put a warning label on those tight pants.

He takes another long drag.

DESTINY: You should quit.

She takes the smoke and stubs it out. He lights another.

JACOB: I've tried. God knows, I've tried.

DESTINY: I don't understand addictions.

JACOB: I'm kind of an expert on the subject. Been through more AA sponsors than I can count. I've done hypnosis, lasers, acupuncture, shiatsu and cold turkey. But I finally found something stronger than booze. *(Holds up the burning cigarette.)* Cigarettes. Been sober eight months since I started smoking. And that's a record for me. If they keep me from drinking, I'll keep smoking.

DESTINY: One form of suicide over another.

JACOB: This one's slower. *(Pause.)* Thanks.

DESTINY: For what?

JACOB: Saving my life. And for sticking around.

DESTINY: Isaac saved your life too. He's running back to the reserve for help. Pumps weren't made for running. Especially in gravel.

JACOB glances at her shoes.

JACOB: Nice. Italian?

DESTINY: They are.

JACOB: Thousand bucks a bit steep for shoes, don't you think?

DESTINY: Not these ones.

JACOB shows his running shoes.

JACOB: Ten bucks. Giant Tiger. Comfy and durable.

DESTINY: That's because they were made by some kid who is chained to his sewing machine in a sweatshop in Vietnam. My shoes were handmade by a cobbler in Venice. He carved a model of my foot. He cured and dyed the leather himself. It took him a week to make these shoes and I paid according to his labour and skill. Yes, they're pricey but no one got exploited making them.

JACOB: Except the cow.

DESTINY: Funny.

JACOB: Don't you think it's ironic that you're going to be making cutbacks to a reserve's finances while you spend a thousand dollars on one pair of shoes.

DESTINY: These are the most comfortable pumps I have ever owned. I don't get cramps in my calves. I don't feel like my ankle is about to break with every step. Ask any woman out there how much she should be paid for standing all day in cheap heels and keeping a smile on her face and she will tell you it's a lot more than a thousand dollars! I can make those decisions, Jacob, because I understand value. I won't buy cheap because someone else always pays for that cheapness—whether it's exploited labour, displaced Indigenous people or non-existent environmental standards. I drive a hybrid. I eat locally grown food. My clothes are not sewn by third world children. I am responsible for every dollar I spend and I spend every dollar responsibly. That's how I roll, bub. And someone who makes their living as a journalist should know that that's not the definition of irony. What's ironic, bub, is that my grandparents were driven off this very reserve because of a corrupt chief and council who had it out for them, and it's me who's coming back to save it from financial ruin! That's fucking ironic! Auuughh!

She sits down. Frustrated.

DESTINY: I didn't need this job. I didn't need this job. I didn't need this job.

She opens her bag and takes out a cleansing shake.

JACOB: I'm sensing you are a little upset—

DESTINY: A little upset?

She opens the drink and starts chugging.

JACOB: Maybe you should talk about it. I've been through a lot of therapy myself. I picked up a thing or two. You seem angry about something.

DESTINY: I'm angry that I took this job when I didn't need it and now I'm stuck here. I need to be in Montreal tomorrow and I'm not sure I'm going to make it. I mean, Indian Affairs begged me to take this job and I kept saying no but the RDG just wouldn't let up. So I took it. As a favour.

JACOB: You mean they had to go all the way to Montreal to get a third party manager?

DESTINY: I'm going to Montreal because my fiancé and I met there three years ago this weekend. I live in Regina.

JACOB: Fiancé?

DESTINY: Yeah. His name is Rick.

JACOB: I don't see a ring.

DESTINY: You won't. Same reason why I won't buy cheap shoes.

JACOB: They're made out of third-world children?

DESTINY: Blood diamonds. Read up on the subject.

JACOB: I know, I know. Africa, child soldiers, corrupt dictators. Blah blah blah.

DESTINY: Blah blah blah?

JACOB: That's why I bought a cubic zirconia. No one's fought a war over them. My ring. Not a real diamond.

DESTINY: Cubic zirconia? You were trying to give me a cubic zirconia as an engagement ring?

JACOB: Well, no child soldiers died getting them.

DESTINY: So your fiancée knew it wasn't a real diamond?

JACOB: If you can't tell the difference—

DESTINY: You didn't tell them!

JACOB: It looks the same! The band is real platin... nomium...

DESTINY: What the hell is "platinomium?"

JACOB: It's practically the same as platinum.

DESTINY: Fake diamond with fake platinum. Good start for any relationship.

JACOB: Hey, at least I'm not funding wars in Africa.

DESTINY: You see Rick wouldn't do that. He's honest and honourable. Hard working. He's the perfect man for me. We have the same values. The same dreams and ambitions.

Pause. She starts crying.

And he left me for some actress! An actress!

JACOB: That's…that's too bad. Maybe you should…you know…move on.

DESTINY: A fucking actress!

JACOB: You see, there's that rage thing I was worried—

DESTINY: What kind of future could they have? Acting is not a secure way to make a living! And actors are not… responsible people.

JACOB: Well, I've never known any—

DESTINY: They're not! He just needs to see that. I know it's just a matter of time. He'll understand she's not right for him. I just need to make sure he sees it that way.

JACOB: So that's why you have to be in Montreal.

DESTINY: I have to be there anyway—I'm setting up a new office. If he wants to see me… He knows my number.

JACOB: Yeah, but does he know you're coming?

DESTINY: He knows.

We hear a truck approaching fast.

JACOB: Is that Isaac?

The truck stops. ISAAC enters running.

ISAAC: How's he doing?

Pause.

Black out.

Scene 4

ISAAC's office on the Reserve, which is in the abandoned residential school. JACOB is holding a portable defibrillator looking at the instructions. An unlit cigarette dangles from his mouth. DESTINY is on the phone talking to the RCMP.

JACOB: *(Reading.)* Portable Automatic Defibrillator.

DESTINY: You wouldn't need that if you just took care of yourself better. *(Into phone.)* Yes, this is Destiny Charles. I need to report an accident or something.

JACOB: That's the beauty of the humankind, isn't it—the smart monkeys create these things so that fat, stupid and lazy monkeys can stay fat, stupid and lazy. Hmmm. I sense a conspiracy.

ISAAC enters.

Here's one of the smart monkeys now.

ISAAC: What are you still doing here? Once those boys get into town they aren't coming back.

JACOB: I don't need to go to the hospital.

DESTINY: *(Into phone.)* On the road south of Thunder Cree. I ran into a dumb monkey driving another vehicle he called Stella.

ISAAC: You're going to the hospital. You just had a heart attack.

JACOB: I'm fine. I was just winded.

DESTINY: *(Into phone.)* No, not a real monkey!

ISAAC: You're not fine.

JACOB: I am so.

DESTINY: *(Into phone.)* I am not making that up!

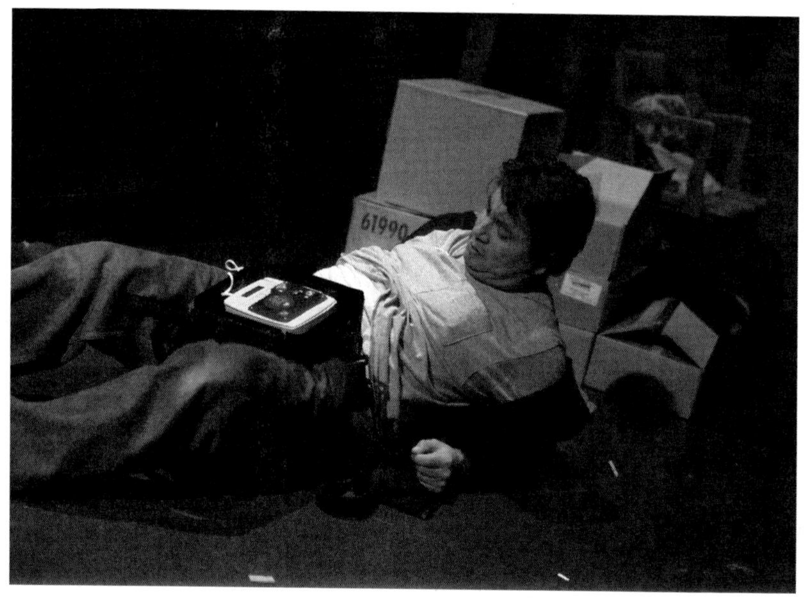

Mark Dieter (Jacob)

ISAAC: Are not.

JACOB: Am so!

ISAAC: Go to the fucking hospital!

JACOB: No!

DESTINY: Boys! Knock it off! *(Calm is restored.)* You're worse than five-year-olds.

JACOB: I'm going outside for a smoke.

He goes outside but not offstage. While the scene continues he smokes and, as he reads the instructions, starts applying the pads from the defibrillator to his chest.

DESTINY: *(Into phone.)* Look, Constable, the other monkey—I mean driver, his name is Jacob Thunderchild…I know I'm not supposed to leave the scene of an accident but there was no way… No, I didn't know road is not used anymore… What!… You're kidding me! *(She slams the phone down.)* Augh! Why did I take this stupid job! *(To ISAAC.)* Does anyone have a tow truck on this reserve?

ISAAC: Closest one is in town.

DESTINY: Great. We have to get our cars off the road or we'll be cited for causing a hazard or something. And we have to go and file an accident report with the cops and S.G.I. and they have to assess the damage AND I HAVE TO BE IN MONTREAL TOMORROW!

ISAAC: What do you mean you didn't need this job?

DESTINY: I'm not in a good mood right now so I don't want to talk about it.

ISAAC: If you don't want to be here, then I'll happily sign off and get down to business getting this community back on its feet.

DESTINY: It doesn't work that way, chum. Whether it's me or somebody else, this reserve is under third-party management as of today. I'm in charge and that's all there is to it. All I needed to do today was let you and the band council know what the score was, get the necessary files and leave. One hour, max. And then I was on my way to Montreal for my anniversary weekend with Rick.

ISAAC: So getting to Montreal was more important than figuring out what help this community needs?

DESTINY: The paperwork usually tells me all I need to know.

ISAAC: What about consulting with the people here? Hearing what they think is important?

DESTINY: That's why I talk to you and the council. You were all elected to represent the community. That's how a democracy works. But if you feel like holding a general meeting and getting their input, fine. Do it. Just be aware that I won't authorize any per diem cheques for them to show up.

ISAAC: We're not like that here.

DESTINY: Then you'd be the first.

ISAAC: Look, I am not one of those chiefs who wants to be chief because it means power. I am here because I want to do the best for the people here. But the system Indian Affairs imposed? I have to deal with housing and financial regulations that contradict themselves—with anonymous bureaucrats who can freeze or delay funding because I haven't filed one of the one hundred and eighty reports that Indian Affairs insists we file. I'm not the first to deal with this stuff or the whims of the various federal governments who say they are committed to making our lives better or reigning us in, but will not listen to us!

DESTINY: You're preaching.

ISAAC: I haven't even started to preach! I lived and worked in Africa for fifteen years as a war correspondent. I saw some really fucked up, evil shit there. Inhumanity borne from desperation—from war or starvation—where a cup of powdered milk meant life or death. Believe me, what people did for that milk was unspeakable. But you can't hate or judge these people because if you were suffering like them you'd do the same. But do you know what's really fucked up? Here, in Canada, we spend seven billion dollars a year to make sure Indian people are impoverished, broken and displaced. We do it through the Indian Act, we do it through Indian Affairs.

By this point JACOB has the defibrillator charged up. It's starts beeping. Alarmed, he tries to turn it off.

DESTINY: The "system" is not meant to keep you down.

ISAAC: If it's not lifting us up, then what is it doing? Where does that money go? It goes to a government department. It goes to the thousands of "consultants" who make a buck off the misery of my people. It goes to third-party managers who don't have to report how much they make to the people of the community.

The defibrillator shocks JACOB, knocking him to the floor. He thrashes and twitches as each shock fires through him.

JACOB: *(Between jolts.)* Help! Help! Ike! Save! Me! Cuz! Zin!

ISAAC picks up the defibrillator and unplugs the pads from the machine.

ISAAC: Jake! You OK? Say something.

JACOB: Just need a minute. *(Takes a deep breath.)* It's just like being tazered.

DESTINY: Cops tazered you?

JACOB: No. My fourth ex-wife. She was really, really, really pissed at me. *(Pats his chest.)* That got the old ticker going.

DESTINY: Singed some of your hair too.

JACOB: As long as I didn't soil myself. I didn't soil myself, did I?

ISAAC: You're fine.

JACOB: Good. That would be a little embarrassing.

ISAAC: Why were you playing with that thing?

JACOB: I wasn't playing, I was planning. Just reading the instructions and then it starts beeping and flashing. Next thing I know… *(He sniffs the air.)* Is someone frying baloney? *(He stands.)* But I feel OK now.

ISAAC: You sure?

JACOB: Never better. I think it helped my posture too.

DESTINY: Look, Chief, is there any place I can stay tonight? I have a feeling I'm going to be here for…longer than I wanted.

JACOB: Yeah. Me too?

ISAAC: Wellll. You both could stay with me.

DESTINY: I could hitch a ride into town or something.

ISAAC: I've got lots of room. I live here.

JACOB: You live in the residential school!

ISAAC: Yes, but in the teachers' part. You'll each have your own room.

DESTINY: You wouldn't happen to have high-speed internet too.

ISAAC: Of course. Hooked it up myself.

DESTINY exits through the building.

JACOB: Wow. I thought you'd want to stay as far away as you could from this place.

ISAAC: When they asked me to run for chief I needed a place to stay on the reserve. And with housing being so tight, I didn't want to take a house from someone. So I just got utilities reconnected and it's fine. It's a solid building. There's nothing wrong with it..

JACOB: Kind of spooky, though.

ISAAC: The ghosts and I have a lot in common. So we usually just chew the shit when they show up.

JACOB: There's ghosts?

ISAAC: No, there aren't any ghosts. Grow up a little.

Black out.

Scene 5

It's late at night. DESTINY is in the living room, doing yoga, following a yoga book in front of her. She's wearing a yoga leotard. She's in the middle of Downward Dog when JACOB ambles by behind her dressed only in his underwear and T-shirt. An unlit cigarette dangles from his mouth. He's carrying a cup. She doesn't see him. He's halfway across the room when he finally spots her. He stops. Stares. And forgetting about the cup, drops it on his foot. It hurts. DESTINY screams and falls out of her pose, grabs the yoga mat and wraps it around her.

DESTINY: Jacob! Get out of here!

JACOB: Sorry, you surprised me.

DESTINY: I'm not the one sneaking around. Put some pants on! Jesus.

JACOB: I was just going for a smoke.

DESTINY: In your underwear?

JACOB: Isaac told me not to smoke inside!

DESTINY: I don't care. Just get lost.

ISAAC enters, sleepy, wearing a housecoat and holding a bat.

ISAAC: What's going on?

JACOB: I was going for a smoke when Stripperella here—

DESTINY: I was doing yoga!

JACOB: In the middle of the night?

DESTINY: I couldn't sleep.

ISAAC: Why aren't you wearing pants?

JACOB: I was being considerate.

ISAAC: Considerate? How is walking around in your gotch "considerate?"

JACOB: I didn't want my clothes to smell of cigarette smoke because I know it bugs you and you know I really need to feed this addiction so if both of you don't mind I'm going outside to smoke this.

JACOB exits.

ISAAC: You couldn't sleep?

DESTINY: No. I saw your yoga book. I didn't think you'd mind.

ISAAC: I don't.

DESTINY: Excuse me a second.

ISAAC: Oh, sorry.

He turns around. DESTINY reaches into one of her bags and pulls out a pair of shorts and quickly puts them on. Then she cracks open yet another cleansing drink and starts gulping it.

DESTINY: You can turn around now.

ISAAC does.

So you're into yoga too?

ISAAC: Yes. My wife got me doing it.

DESTINY: Wife?

ISAAC: Late wife. She died ten years ago.

DESTINY: Oh I'm sorry.

ISAAC: It's OK. You, uh, are you supposed to drink those that often?

DESTINY: I'm on a cleanse.

ISAAC: A cleanse?

DESTINY: Getting rid of the toxins in my body. Flushing out the system. Giving it a reboot. Tell me about your wife.

ISAAC: Zia.

DESTINY: That's an interesting name.

ISAAC: She was born in Iran but her family fled during the Islamic revolution. I met her in South Africa. She was working for CNN. I was shooting for some European newspapers. My portfolio is around here somewhere.

He spots the portfolio and hands it to her. She looks through the pages.

DESTINY: Oh my god! Where was this?

ISAAC: Rwanda. That's a Tutsi man begging for his life. He was hiding in a truck but got caught at a Hutu checkpoint. He was murdered a few minutes later. By those guys with the machetes.

DESTINY: How scary was that?

ISAAC: Very. It never stopped being scary. But these were things that shouldn't be ignored. I felt I had a responsibility to tell their stories. This one man tells the story of the 800,000 who were murdered. It would be a shame if we forgot this man.

DESTINY: You witnessed some intense stuff.

ISAAC: Yeah, we did. Me and Zia, I mean.

DESTINY turns a page.

DESTINY: Whoa. That's uhhh...that's a little weird. That woman could be my twin sister.

ISAAC: That's Zia.

DESTINY: Zia.

She closes the portfolio and hands it back.

ISAAC: So you see it too?

DESTINY: How can I not see it? To be honest, my stomach has a funny feeling right now.

ISAAC: Yeah, mine too.

DESTINY: I don't know if I want to know but... what was she like?

He opens the portfolio.

ISAAC: Here. I'll show you. This photo here was taken in the West Bank during the first Intifada. So let me set this up. She's arguing with these soldiers at this checkpoint. They're not letting the media in. And before we can look for another route in, she's in their faces, screaming at them in Hebrew. They're screaming back. It gets very intense and then this officer just pops her in the head with the butt of his rifle.

DESTINY: Oh my god, what did you do?

ISAAC: I took that picture.

DESTINY: You jerk!

ISAAC: If I hadn't then she would've been ten times pissed at me. You wanted to know what she was like—that's what she was like. And she laughed about it later. Because she got them. If they do that to us, the media, especially to an Israeli journalist, imagine what they're doing to the Palestinians. Passionate. Professional. Smart. Oh man, she was smart. She spoke at least eight languages.

Pause.

She wanted to come here with me. "I want to see where your home is." It's a reserve, why would I want to come back? "Because you can and I can't. I can never return to Iran. To my real home." Remember that?

DESTINY: Pardon.

ISAAC: Sorry. Sorry.

He closes the book.

DESTINY: It's OK.

ISAAC: When I saw you by the road, I thought I saw a

ghost. And looking at these pictures… I miss her so much. I can't believe how much I still miss her.

Pause. She puts her arm around his shoulders.

DESTINY: You're going to be OK.

JACOB re-enters, sees them and freezes.

JACOB: Ahem!

ISAAC and DESTINY jump.

DESTINY: Ah Jesus Jacob, you scared me.

JACOB: How long has this been going on?

ISAAC: What are you talking about?

JACOB: What am I talking about? You seem pretty lovey-dovey, that's what I'm talking about! I go for a smoke and you two are wrapped in each other's arms.

DESTINY: We were not.

JACOB: Were too.

DESTINY: Were not!

ISAAC: We were talking about Zia, dumbass!

JACOB: Ooooh, the old "dead wife" scenario. Used it myself. Very effective.

ISAAC: You don't have any dead wives!

JACOB: That's why I know it works! *(To DESTINY.)* You must be pretty weak-willed by now. All warmed up by his sadness. Thinking, OK, a wife means he's not afraid of commitment. A dead wife means he's available. I know how you women are. I've married enough of you.

DESTINY: Jacob…

JACOB: Yeah?

DESTINY: Oh fuck it!

Faster than lightning, she punches JACOB in the jaw, knocking him into ISAAC's arms.

JACOB: Smoke break!

Black out.

Scene 6

JACOB and ISAAC are sitting outside the teachers' quarters. JACOB is holding a bag of ice to his chin. We can see DESTINY in the background, wearing a headset, working on her computer.

JACOB: I'm sorry I barged in like that. I didn't know what the plan was. And I thought you knew I had the hots for her. I should've called dibs or something. But it's totally my fault for not letting you know. Just to be clear, I don't blame you for this. Next time, just give me a heads up and I'll stay out of the way.

JACOB pops a smoke into his mouth and searches for the lighter.

She's hot. Totally understand the attraction. And I'm not the cock-blocking type. Especially with family. What time is it anyway?

ISAAC shows him his watch.

She's got a fiancé, you know. Rick. Well, a fiancé in her mind anyway. She tell you about that yet? Totally fucked up. That's why she's going to Montreal. He's there, shacking up with some actress. She's all messed up about that.

Pause.

OK, fine, don't talk to me.

DESTINY is drinking a cleansing shake.

DESTINY: Pick up pick up. Come on.

She sees ISAAC'S portfolio and opens it.

Rick, it's Destiny. I know you see the 1-800 number, but it's me on my internet phone. I'm going to call back in a few minutes. Please pick up.

She disconnects. She finishes her cleansing drink. She looks at the empty can.

Why do I keep drinking this shit? He's got to have something more powerful around.

She does a quick scan of ISAAC's cupboards but finds nothing. Suddenly an idea hits her.

Jacob.

She exits. Back to ISAAC and JACOB.

ISAAC: What does this place mean to you, Jake?

JACOB looks at the school.

JACOB: It's an empty building. It means nothing.

ISAAC: Nothing?

JACOB: Nothing.

ISAAC: My mom and dad were sent here. Our aunts, uncles. Our grandparents. Our great-grandparents. Cousins. Me. *(Beat.)* Your dad. It must mean something.

Pause. JACOB tosses his smoke and lights another.

JACOB: What it means to me now took a lot of painful work—a lot of forgiving and a lot forgetting. So now, really, honestly and truthfully, this building is just a building.

ISAAC: The feds have offered to erase the band's debt if we knock down the school.

JACOB: Really?

ISAAC: And they'll build a brand new, state-of-the-art school.

JACOB: And? There's got to be some sort of catch.

ISAAC: Oh there's a catch—Saskatchewan's last residential school building will be nothing but a fading memory.

JACOB: Maybe it should be.

ISAAC: Israel has Yed Vesham, their Holocaust memorial. They seek out and collect as many artifacts and stories of the Shoah as they can, no matter how painful. Baby shoes, empty suitcases, death camp uniforms, diaries, even barbed wire. They cling to those physical reminders of the worst moment of their history. Yet from that pain, they gained the strength to build their nation.

JACOB: Keeping this building will not give us strength. Take the money. Tear it down.

ISAAC: Money won't fix the problems here.

JACOB: It'll get you out of debt and rid of the third-party manager. Or do you want her sticking around?

ISAAC: I don't want this band under third-party management. But how are we supposed to heal if we don't understand why we're hurting in the first place. This school tried to eradicate us. Not with gas chambers but by kidnapping us and making us strangers to our own parents. This school was a factory to eliminate the Indian and cast us adrift into the wind.

DESTINY returns with two bottles of mixed unknown booze. She opens one, sniffs it and recoils. She opens the other, sniff, hmmmm, not so bad. She gets herself a glass and pours a shot. She has a taste. Hey, that's actually not bad at all. She slugs it.

DESTINY: Oh yeah! Come to mama!

She pours some more, dials the number, waits and gets voicemail.

Oh come on, Rick, you got my message, you saw my number and you know it's me. *(Voicemail again.)* Hey Rick, it's Destiny, look, OK, ummmm, I know things didn't go as we planned. But hey, let's uhhhhh, let's uhhhh... God, why am I so flustered... hehehehehe, yeah, I'm talking to myself... I don't want you to think— Look, I called because I won't be in Montreal this Saturday. Maybe later, you know, like Sunday. But I was wondering you know if we could get together, have a coffee, I mean. I'll be there for a little while. Montreal I mean, so if Sunday's not good, we could make it Monday... or Tuesday...or Wednesday... well,you know the rest of the week. I'm blabbering I'm blabbering, I know I know. Sorry, I know how much you don't like it when I do that.

She disconnects.

Goddamnit!

She slugs back the drink and pours herself a much stronger one.

I am not a stalker.

She drinks a sip.

I am not. *(Sip.)* A stalker.

Another sip. Then dials the number again. She waits, she sips, she waits, she sips, voicemail again.

Hey Rick, Destiny. I must've hit a button accidentally or something. You know these internet connections. Can be a little unreliable. Especially on reserve. That's where I'm calling from. A reserve. Thunder Cree actually. That's not important. Again, I'll be in Montreal soon. Or Mon-real, as the locals like to call it. I've been working on my French. And I've taken up yoga. I'm trying some different styles—Hatha, Ashtanga Vinyasa, Six Lokas, even Hothouse Kundalini Laughter Yoga. I'm eating better. Drinking those special drinks you always liked. Can we just talk? Face to face. Just once? Just, you know, so we could see if could patch things up. Think about it. I'll call you when I get there.

She thinks she disconnects.

Oh yeah. That non-blood diamond ring is as good as mine.

She realizes the computer is still on and punches the off button then pours a shot, slugs it, and stares at her hand admiring the imagined engagement ring. She pours a much bigger shot. Back to ISAAC and JACOB.

JACOB: So let me get this straight—you went to residential school yet you want to keep the building? But to keep it, you have to keep the band in debt?

ISAAC: Actually, I don't.

JACOB: You don't. How?

ISAAC: I can erase the band's debt.

JACOB: The government's stepping in, I can't see how.

ISAAC: I mean, I, personally, can erase the debt. I have the money myself.

JACOB: You've been ripping off band funds!

ISAAC: I haven't been— why would you think that?

JACOB: You're the chief.

ISAAC: Even you?

JACOB: Sorry man. It just slipped out.

ISAAC: Because it's a stereotype we accept without question. It's a sign of hopelessness. If we believe these things without question then—

JACOB: OK, fair enough. I know you're not a thief. But some previous chiefs…

ISAAC: Walk a mile in my moccassins, cousin. You'll see different. It's easy to piss on the leaders when that's all you do is piss and moan. Chief Charlie begged me to run for chief. "We need your moniyaw smarts," he said. "Maybe you can figure out these strange rules and regulations for funding that keep changing and shifting." I had no idea. Some fucking good I'm doing. But I could get this band out of its debt without destroying the school.

JACOB: How?

ISAAC: I inherited a lot of money when Zia died.

JACOB: How much money?

ISAAC: Enough to write a cheque for the band's debt.

JACOB: Why don't you?

ISAAC: Would you?

JACOB: Yes.

ISAAC: OK, I'll start with whatever you got in your wallet.

JACOB: I don't have your kind of money.

ISAAC: Consider it an investment.

JACOB: Are you kidding?

ISAAC: Exactly. The system is fucked. Even you won't put five bucks into it. And if I pay off the band's debt, that's it. No more inheritance. Zia's legacy is done. And if I'm going to spend it, I want to make sure it goes to something meaningful—something that she would be proud of. I'm just hoping I can work something out with Destiny.

JACOB: I knew it. You have the hots for her.

ISAAC: Shut up, or I'll punch the other side of your face.

ISAAC and JACOB enter the building. DESTINY puts the bottle down and she takes a sip. Pause.

DESTINY: You wouldn't happen to have a little mix, would you? This stuff is a little harsh?

JACOB: My booze!

JACOB runs and grabs the bottle. It's now nearly half empty.

DESTINY: Relax, I'm a girl who can handle her liquor.

ISAAC: Are you OK?

DESTINY: Ducky.

JACOB sniffs the bottle.

ISAAC: What was in that bottle?

JACOB: Uhhhm...one-five-one...plus some other stuff.

DESTINY: And it's yummy. Gimme.

She reaches for the bottle. ISAAC pulls it away.

DESTINY: Hey! Don't make me come over there.

ISAAC: I think you've had enough.

DESTINY: Fucking men, always think they fucking know better.

She pulls a mickey that she's hidden in the back of her yoga pants. JACOB reaches the bottle. They scuffle. JACOB wins but spills it all out.

JACOB: Nooooooo! This isn't happening this isn't happening this isn't happening!

DESTINY: Oopsie.

JACOB: You fucking cow! I was saving those for a special occasion!

She runs to ISAAC for protection but when she looks at him…

DESTINY: Rick! Fuck you, Rick! I keep trying to forget you but you keep creeping back in like a worm, chewing at my brain, bite by tiny, irritating minuscule bite. You are a worm. That's what you are. A worm! No, no, not just a worm. You are the snot that runs from the worm's nose. Infectious, bacteria-ridden worm snot that leaves a trail of sickly slime everywhere it goes. That's you, buddy. That's you.

ISAAC: Rick?

She realizes it's ISAAC.

DESTINY: And you? Do you know why I came here? Why, even though I really didn't need the money or the hassle, I came back here…

ISAAC: For revenge?

DESTINY: Revenge! Fuck you! Smartass. You think you have all the answers, don't you? But you don't. I do. I have the answers.

Curtis Peeteetucer (Isaac) and Paula Jean Prudat (Destiny)

She collapses into his arms.

ISAAC: OK, OK, I think you need a lie down.

DESTINY: I'm not lying down. I'm finally standing up! That's right, up. For myself. For my family. Against men like you who keep trying to keep me down. Because you can't stand to see a successful Cree woman make something of herself!

She pukes onto ISAAC's chest. Pause. She stares dreamily into his eyes.

Marry me, stud lover!

She plants a kiss on ISAAC. They are locked in this embrace as the lights go down.

End of Act I.

Act II

Scene 1

Lights up in ISAAC's living room. DESTINY is asleep on the couch. A bag of frozen spinach on her head, a bucket next to her. The laptop sits open on the floor. It plays an eight-bit version of a Rick Astley song—or any other pop song that reminds you of metal fingernails scratching a chalkboard. The song plays and plays.

ISAAC: *(O.S.)* Destiny. *(Louder.)* Destiny! *(Waits. Louder.)* Destiny! Your stupid computer alarm is making that noise again!

Pause. DESTINY doesn't move.

(O.S.) Oh Christ!

He enters, half asleep he stubs his toe. The Rick Astley song attracts his attention again and he finds the computer and turns it off. He scans the messages quickly.

Restraining order?

He closes the computer. JACOB enters.

Where you been?

JACOB: Out walking. Thinking. Looking for a pack of smokes. No smoke shacks on this rez, eh?

ISAAC: Nope. Gas station opens in a couple hours.

JACOB: Don't know if I can hold out that long. You'd think after eight months that need would go away.

ISAAC: What are you talking about?

JACOB: Smoking keeps me sober.

ISAAC: You're kidding me.

JACOB: Wish I was. *(He looks around the room.)* Ike?

ISAAC: Yeah?

JACOB: Was I hallucinating or was Rick Astley singing all morning?

ISAAC: You weren't hallucinating.

JACOB: OK, good. Hallucinations are not a good sign. Especially, when you need to drink. I need to know what I'm seeing is actually there and not my brain jonesing for a fix. So don't look at me funny when I ask why. Destiny has a bag of spinach on her face?

ISAAC: She has what?

He looks. He lifts the bag. The spinach has thawed and a green slimy goop drips all over her face. This wakes her.

Ah, you're finally…

She turns and hurls into the bucket.

Up.

She tries to focus on ISAAC.

DESTINY: Kill me.

She becomes semi-aware of the thawed spinach.

ISAAC: I'll get you some water.

She heaves.

DESTINY: Drowning won't work. I'm a really good swimmer.

ISAAC: *(To JACOB.)* If you need motivation not to drink. Take a good look at her.

He exits. She heaves again.

JACOB: Nope. Not working. Not working at all. I need a drink.

ISAAC returns with a washcloth and a glass of water. She gulps the water down and he starts cleaning off the spinach. She smiles.

DESTINY: How do I look?

ISAAC: Beautiful.

DESTINY: Really?

ISAAC: Yep. You might need more of those cleansing drinks. You re-toxified yourself pretty good last night.

He finishes wiping her face.

There. Good as new.

She hurls.

(To JACOB.) You think you can mix together some of your hangover cure.

JACOB: Do you have the ingredients?

ISAAC: Do your best.

JACOB looks around the place, randomly mixing ingredients into a mug. DESTINY feels the spinach on her clothes and hair.

DESTINY: I'm turning green!

ISAAC: That's frozen spinach.

DESTINY: You put frozen spinach on me? Why?

ISAAC: I didn't do it. You must've or Jacob.

JACOB: I didn't do it. Maybe Rick Astley did.

DESTINY: Who the hell freezes spinach anyway?

ISAAC: Hey! It's hard to get fresh groceries on the reserve.

JACOB offers DESTINY the mug.

JACOB: Drink this. It'll help.

She sniffs it.

DESTINY: What is it?

JACOB: Ahhh, it's some uhhh…it's best you didn't know. I had to improvise. I didn't have my hangover kit with me.

DESTINY: You have a hangover kit?

JACOB: Every drunk has a hangover kit. Drink up, boozehound.

DESTINY: I'm not a boozehound.

She drinks back the mug. The laptop starts playing that song again.

DESTINY: Oh my god, that's Rick! I got a message from Rick.

ISAAC: I wouldn't bother. It's not good news.

DESTINY: You read my messages!

She stands up, grabs the bucket and staggers to her computer.

ISAAC: You left it open and it plays that annoying Rick Astley song when he messages you.

DESTINY: That's our song.

She reads the messages.

DESTINY: A restraining order? He doesn't know what he's talking about. I just need to see him once and clear this up. There's got to be a flight out to Montreal today.

She starts tapping at the keyboard.

ISAAC: Wait a minute. You've got business with us first.

DESTINY: It can wait. This is my future husband we're talking about. Hey, how far are we from Edmonton?

ISAAC: Edmonton? Look, he's made it pretty clear—

DESTINY: There's a flight leaving in four hours.

ISAAC: Rick doesn't want to see you.

DESTINY: Once he sees me, he'll know he's making a big mistake.

ISAAC: His last message said "don't make me call the police." All caps. Exclamation mark.

DESTINY: It's probably that damn actress who wrote that.

JACOB: Ever thought of letting him move on with his life?

She gives him the finger.

DESTINY: Ever thought of minding your own fucking business!

JACOB shrugs and exits.

ISAAC: You know, there are laws against this.

DESTINY: I'm not a stalker!

ISAAC: Then what difference does it make if you go there today or tomorrow or next week?

DESTINY: He neeeeeeds—

She hurls into the bucket.

...me.

ISAAC: So much for the hangover mix.

DESTINY: Can I have some more water please?

ISAAC gets her a glass of water.

DESTINY: Rick's not going to let go of me that easily. I've invested too much energy in molding him into the husband of my dreams.

ISAAC hands her the glass. She drinks.

That's the thing about you guys, you don't understand. How much work you require. The weeks and months we women put into making sure you can eat right, know how to pick the right paint swatches to match the tile samples, getting the right job. You think that happens overnight? It doesn't. It takes a hell of a lot of commitment because you're sure as hell are not born that way. Two years I worked on Rick. He was all jeans and rugby shirts when I met him. I'm not letting a little thing like a restraining order get in the way of that. Who can I call to get a ride to Edmonton?

ISAAC: In your condition?

DESTINY: I'll be fine when I get to the airport. Come on, chop chop. Get the word out. I need to get to Edmonton and I'll pay. Like now.

ISAAC: You have to file—

DESTINY: I don't care about stupid police reports. I just want to see Rick!

JACOB returns with the remaining liquor bottles.

JACOB: Ike. Get rid of these for me.

ISAAC: Jake?

JACOB: I'm out of smokes and I really, really need a fucking drink and if you don't pour these down the sink right now I'm going to fucking swallow these down one after the other.

ISAAC: You sure?

JACOB: Right now.

ISAAC quickly grabs the bottles and exits. JACOB is breathing heavy.

JACOB: *(To himself.)* I can't fucking win. I can't fucking win.

ISAAC re-enters.

ISAAC: Is that it, Jake? You haven't got more stashed anywhere?

JACOB: No.

ISAAC: Do I need to get help?

JACOB: I can't fucking win, Ike! I CAN'T FUCKING WIN! EIGHT FUCKING MONTHS AND I CAN'T STOP! I NEED A FUCKING DRINK! I need a fucking drink, Ike. I need to drink. I need to drink. I need a fucking drink.

JACOB collapses. ISAAC grabs his cousin and holds him.

I need a fucking drink. I need a fucking drink. I can't fucking win. I can't win. I can't win.

Black out.

Scene 2

JACOB and DESTINY are sitting outside of the teachers' quarters. JACOB has a smoke. DESTINY has an icepack on the back of her head. ISAAC is inside talking on the phone. Pause.

JACOB: I'm sorry you saw that.

DESTINY: It's all right. I'm sorry I told you to mind your own business.

JACOB: I think you said, mind your own "fucking" business.

DESTINY: With this.

She gives him the finger. They laugh.

And honestly, who freezes spinach?

JACOB: My cousin, that's who. And I can't believe he's living here, of all places.

DESTINY: Did you go here?

JACOB: No. Isaac did. I went to the day school in town.

DESTINY: How come Isaac didn't go?

JACOB: He was an orphan—church claimed him pretty quick. The principal told Indian Affairs he was now under his care.

DESTINY: No family could take him?

JACOB: Jesus, no! Only family he had was me and my dad. And Wild wasn't father of the year material.

DESTINY: Wild?

JACOB: His rez name. Dad's real name was Ignatius, or Iggy. He hated that name.

DESTINY: Ignatius?

JACOB: My grandparents were sent to the Catholic school in Lebret. So they named all their kids after saints and popes. Isaac's dad was named Innocent. Then there was Pius, Augustine, Magdalena and Boniface.

DESTINY: So you have lots of family around here.

JACOB: Nope. Pius killed himself, Augustine drank himself to death, Magdalena was murdered and Uncle Boniface got run over by a train. Innocent was killed in a car accident with Isaac's mother. Me and Isaac are the last Thunderchilds on this reserve.

DESTINY: Really? There are lots of other Thunderchilds across the province.

JACOB: They're not related. When they did the treaty rolls they mistranslated my great-great granddad's name and it stuck. My dad tried explaining it to me but he was always too deep in the bag for me to listen. That's the only time he tried to speak Cree to me—when he was pissed. Really turned me off the language. Can't hear it without seeing that pathetic, broken man—so drunk he can't get out of his chair—smelling of shit. "Ash-tum, boy, ash-tum. Ash-tum, fucker! Mee-sis! Wah-pah-gah-mah-how! Aaaaaah ah-was! Fucker!" That was it. My dad teaching me Cree.

DESTINY: I'm sorry.

JACOB: Wasn't your fault. It took a lot for me to stop hating that bastard. Then it took a lot more to stop hating the fuckers who did that to him. It's amazing the kind of shit you can do when you're "saving" someone. *(He searches for a smoke.)* I wish I had a smoke.

DESTINY: Me too.

JACOB: Thought you were more of a…

DESTINY: Health nut?

JACOB: Fitness type.

DESTINY: I am. Well…most of the time. I just need a cigarette today. Fucking Rick.

JACOB: How you feeling?

DESTINY: Like shit. I won't drink like that again…for awhile. Did I get all the spinach out?

He looks her over.

JACOB: I think so.

She tries to drink the shake again but can't.

DESTINY: You want this?

He takes it and sniffs it. Smells good. He takes a sip.

JACOB: Hmmmm. Not bad.

DESTINY: I got six more inside if you want. I don't want them anymore.

JACOB: No more clean living for you?

DESTINY: It's all hard drinking and drugs from now on. Even going to give up yoga. Just sit on my ass all day and play video games and wait for the diabetes to kick in.

JACOB: Sounds like fun. Maybe I'll join you. You have more of these inside?

She nods. He exits to get another drink. ISAAC joins DESTINY.

ISAAC: OK. I got most of the band council lined up for a meeting this afternoon.

DESTINY: Most?

ISAAC: There's a sale on DVD players at the Walmart in

North Battleford. We're lucky to have enough for quorum.

DESTINY: Did you tell them why there was a meeting?

ISAAC: Yes.

DESTINY: And they're still going to Walmart?

ISAAC: They all seemed to know it's coming.

DESTINY: So just accept it?

ISAAC: You're the one who told me we didn't have a say in the matter.

DESTINY: At least care to show up and say something. You see, this is why I stopped doing these kinds of meetings. Used to do them all the time in the beginning but the apathy finally wore me down.

ISAAC: I got most of them.

DESTINY: Isaac, "most" isn't good enough.

ISAAC: I can't horsewhip them into showing up.

DESTINY: Things are going to get tough around here. Programs are going to get cut.

ISAAC: You think I don't know that.

DESTINY: Instead they're off buying cheap DVD players. That tells me so much about why this place is in the mess that's it in.

ISAAC: It's just a DVD player.

DESTINY: It's not just a DVD player, it's a symptom of a bigger problem. Is that DVD player going to cut down on the health problems here? The unemployment? Is it going to guarantee more high school grads? Are people going to exercise more? Will they eat better? Will they stop smoking? It's like why we need to buy defibrillators. They're just band aids and wouldn't be necessary if our people exercised, quit smoking or ate right. God, I can't keep seeing this over and over again. You're lucky you got this school. I can at least get the debt erased quickly.

ISAAC: Lucky to have this school? Do you have a clue what happened here?

DESTINY: All I care about now is your financial future. Not your past.

ISAAC: This is history. A sad part of history that the government is trying to sweep under the carpet. Once this building goes there will no physical reminders of what happened here. As if the lives that were ruined here meant nothing.

DESTINY: Oh please. Not everyone who went to this school was abused.

ISAAC: What do you call the forced separation of children from their parents? I was actually lucky I was an orphan because I never had to live with the agony of knowing my parents lived just over that hill but were forbidden to ever see me. You know what that does to a kid? That's not only abuse, that's genocide. This building is the last residential school in the province. It must stand as a memorial.

DESTINY: It's not your decision, Chief. Funding is tied to its destruction.

ISAAC: And that doesn't bother you? Make you wonder why that is?

DESTINY: What bothers me is that you'd rather hold this community hostage in a state of financial crisis than get rid of a building that stirs up bad memories.

ISAAC: I'm thinking about its future. For my people to thrive they've got to understand their past.

DESTINY: They're my people too, Chief! And do you think that when our great-grand parents were thinking about the future this is what they dreamed for—obesity, black mold and cheap DVD players?

ISAAC: They didn't have control of their futures. The government took that. Like you're doing.

JACOB returns with a cleansing drink.

DESTINY: If these people had enough "control" to get in a fucking truck and buy some disposable, piece of crap DVD player then they have enough "control" to change their own futures.

JACOB: I had one of those really cheap DVD players and the first thing to break was the remote control. And they don't put buttons on the front anymore. So if you don't have the remote the whole stupid thing is useless. And you just can't go and buy a replaceable remote. You have to buy the whole package again. I don't know how many of those things I've bought. And it's cheaper to buy another than to fix it.

ISAAC and DESTINY glare at him.

Just saying…

JACOB retreats.

ISAAC: Then what do you suggest? What magic, "outside the box" thinking do you have?

DESTINY: You really want to know?

ISAAC: You have a good idea about what's wrong. Tell us what you'd do to make it right.

DESTINY: A vegetable garden.

ISAAC: A what?

DESTINY: A vegetable garden. It provides exercise, healthy food and financial independence in one, neat package. People who garden are fitter, emotionally happier and eat better. It's done wonders for me.

ISAAC: Christ, what were you like before?

DESTINY: You don't want to know, smart ass. I'm Buddha compared to what I was like before.

ISAAC: Buddha?

DESTINY: Fucking Nirvana, baby.

ISAAC: Because of a garden?

DESTINY: You got to start somewhere. You wouldn't have to freeze your spinach anymore. *(Pause.)* It's bugging you that you didn't come up with it, isn't it?

ISAAC: Yeah. Kinda.

DESTINY: So what? You're not used to a girl being smarter than you?

ISAAC: I'm not used to anyone being smarter than me. Except one person.

DESTINY: You are an arrogant jerk.

ISAAC: Fine. I'm arrogant. Doesn't mean I'm wrong.

DESTINY: Except when I'm around.

ISAAC: Who's being arrogant now?

DESTINY: Fine. Doesn't mean I'm wrong either.

ISAAC: You know, I was asked to run by the last chief. He figured I could do a better job than him.

DESTINY: Man, you have a high opinion of yourself. You think maybe he got you elected because he knew third-party was coming? Doesn't matter how bad it was when you got in, all people around here are going to remember is that it was under your watch I took over—that the hard times began. The old chief played you, my friend.

ISAAC: He did not. *(A realization.)* Oh Christ! I can't believe he did that to me. I didn't take a house. I'm not taking a salary. What the fuck am I doing here?

DESTINY: You're not taking a salary? What are you living on?

ISAAC: I got an inheritance when my wife died. Listen to this—I was even considering paying off the band's debt with it.

DESTINY: Isaac Thunderchild…you are something else.

ISAAC: I feel like such a fucking idiot.

DESTINY: OK, come on now. You got played. Look. You're probably the smartest guy I've met. Definitely the smartest chief. And you really care about this place and the people here. As long as you're chief, I'll work with you on getting this band back on track.

ISAAC: Work with me?

DESTINY: Like partners.

JACOB comes back with a cleansing drink.

JACOB: Where do I buy more of these? They're awesome.

Black out.

Scene 3

JACOB, in the living room. He's on the phone with his boss. He's drinking a cleansing shake.

JACOB: Yes, I'm drinking but it's not what you think. Don't worry, I'm not driving… It's a cleansing shake… Cleansing! A naturopathic cleansing shake meant to restore balance… Ba-lance!… Because I crashed the car… My car! Stella!… Because I liked the name Stella, look, it's not important, but I've got a better story for you… No, it was last week… Was so!… Was so!… I'm here, bozo, I know the graduation was last week… OK, OK, sorry about "Bozo" but I've got a better story… Thunder Cree is about to be put under third-party management and… What do you mean, "What's that?" It's when Indian Affairs feels the band can't control their spending and imposes a manager to take over, but here's the real scoop… no, the chief is not corrupt… No! He's not taking bribes, the story is about how— let me finish!… It's more complicated than that… Come on, that's not what the story—the story is about how a chief is trying to get finances under control but doesn't want to demolish the old residential school building just to get the band out of debt… It is not too complicated…these things are never simple… because they're not… OK, OK, so someone with a Grade Six education might have a little trouble understanding it but it's an important issue in our communities… Well fuck you then! If you're so worried about making stories accessible to a grade six audience why the fuck did you send me to cover a Grade Twelve graduation! Ever thought of that, you fucking moron!

He slams the phone down. DESTINY enters.

DESTINY: What's wrong with you?

JACOB: My boss is an idiot.

DESTINY: What is it you do again? You're some sort of reporter or something?

JACOB: I am a video-journalist. Or was. Who knows now. I used to work for APTN National News. *(She shrugs.)* The Aboriginal Peoples Television Network? We have a nightly newscast.

DESTINY: Is that before or after all the throat-singing and seal hunting?

JACOB: We have a great diversity of programming now. We show *The Beachcombers* in Mi'kmaq now. We cut seal hunting by fifty percent. And the news is in English and French.

DESTINY: Well, you don't want all that colonialism to go to waste.

JACOB: You should talk. You seem finely assimilated.

DESTINY: What choice did I have? My grandparents were kicked off this reserve for being "troublemakers" because they wouldn't vote for the chief. Left here with nothing but their clothes. Even so, they didn't let me forget who I am and where I can from. No band council or federal government can take that away from me. I am a Cree woman. Nehiyaw-isquayo. *[Cree]*

JACOB: You speak Cree?

DESTINY: Ey-ha. *[Cree] (Pause.)* Ap-sees. *[Cree]* I took some courses in university. Still see that broken old man now?

JACOB: Only when I look in a mirror.

DESTINY: What is it with you guys feeling sorry for yourselves?

JACOB: I don't feel sorry for myself. I am super thankful for each day I have and every day I'm sober. Some days are better than others. When I say I see that broken old man, it's not that I think I'm turning into him. It's because I know I'm not. Even when I was deep in the booze I was never mean or evil like him. But he's always there. I see his eyes more and more. I tell him I love him.

DESTINY: Really?

JACOB: He did the best he could as a father. He really, really sucked at it. But he did his best. Hating him serves no purpose. My boss on the other hand. Sucking the farts out of dead seagulls would be too good for him. Stupid fucker.

DESTINY: Then why work there?

JACOB: It wasn't always like that. I used to research and pitch my own stories. Not anymore. The new assignment editor assigns us everything. I had a great story idea and he just told me to fuck off.

DESTINY: Which was?

JACOB: Well…have you ever wondered why there are no thirteenth floors?

DESTINY: Superstition?

JACOB: Yeah, but why no thirteenth floor in government buildings? What reason does a government have to be superstitious? They're hiding something.

DESTINY: Like what?

JACOB: I dunno. But the only way to find out is to investigate.

DESTINY: Investigate who? The CIA? Aliens? The Elevator Manufacturer's Cabal for World Domination?

JACOB: Worse.

DESTINY: Worse?

He looks around all paranoid-like. He motions her closer.

JACOB: The Assembly of First Nations. They're involved. I know it.

DESTINY: And you call your boss an idiot?

JACOB: Don't be sarcastic. It's unbecoming. And he's not

my boss anymore. Maybe it's time for a career change.

DESTINY: Yeah, me too. But I would miss that feeling. When I look into the eyes of those corrupt chiefs and councils when they realize I'm in charge. I really like cutting their expense claims and per diems. God I love cutting their per diems. Mmmm-mm-mm-mm-mm-mm. Makes me quiver thinking about it. Revenge tastes awfully sweet.

JACOB: I don't think that's healthy.

DESTINY: Probably not. But it pays well. Why are you a reporter?

JACOB: Not for the money, that's for sure. There ain't any. It's because of Isaac. When I got to college, nothing really interested me. But whenever the old man saw a photo in the newspaper that Isaac took, he'd cut it out and tape it to the fridge. And the chance to travel too. Isaac was reporting from all over Africa. I wanted a piece of that action. It would get me the hell away from here.

DESTINY: Ever make it to Africa?

JACOB: No. Got to Ottawa though. That's something like a success. I guess. I've been clinging to one reporter gig after another. Newspapers. Radio. Now TV. I've failed in all three. Funny thing is, this time, I'm not really bothered if I do lose this job. It feels kinda free, you know. Like a huge weight has been lifted from my shoulders. I can now truly do what I want. The future is full of options.

DESTINY: So what now?

Pause. JACOB picks up the phone and quickly re-dials.

JACOB: Beg for my job back! *(Into phone.)* Assignment please.

DESTINY disconnects the phone.

What are you doing!

DESTINY: What are you doing?

JACOB: I need structure. Order. Discipline. Freedom's not good for my health. I can't handle it. Please plug the phone back in.

DESTINY: You just said it sucks. That a weight has been lifted from your shoulders.

JACOB: My shoulders need that weight. God, I think my back is cramping up. I'm cramping up!

He twists and contorts to the imagined "pain."

DESTINY: Relax!

JACOB: My legs! I can't feel my legs!

DESTINY: Deep breaths deep breaths deep breaths.

She mimics deep breathing for him.

JACOB: Yoga? After my heart attack, you're telling me to do yoga!

DESTINY: Stop panicking, you big baby!

JACOB: I am not panicking. I am taking stock of my situation. God, I can't breathe. The defibrillator? Where's the defibrillator!

DESTINY: Are you having a heart attack?

JACOB: Lemme check?

He grabs his chest.

Seems like it!

He drops to the ground, twisting and writhing.

Zap me! Quick!

DESTINY scrambles to find the defibrillator.

DESTINY: Where did you leave it?

JACOB: Bedroom!

DESTINY runs to his bedroom.

Hurry! I…can't…breathe…

She returns with the P.A.D.

Dizzy.

She quickly pulls the pads out, rips his shirt off and applies them to his chest. The defibrillator beeps.

That means fire.

She zaps him. He twitches.

Again!

She reads the instructions.

DESTINY: It says I'm supposed to wait.

JACOB: Just fire it again!

She fires it again. He twitches and jumps, then stops.

Ahhhhhhh. That's the stuff.

He farts. She waves it away.

DESTINY: God, take it easy with those goji berries.

JACOB: Sorry.

DESTINY: Feeling better?

JACOB: Perfect. We got to stop meeting like this. People will talk.

DESTINY: I think you enjoyed that.

JACOB: A beautiful woman inflicting pain? What's not to love?

DESTINY: You need help for that.

JACOB: One addiction at a time.

DESTINY: We need to take you to the hospital.

JACOB: I'm fine as long as I have this around. *(Taps the defibrillator.)* I think I'll call you Stella Jr.

DESTINY: Stella Jr.?

JACOB: What's wrong with Stella Jr.?

DESTINY: It's not the name…it's…you know, you wouldn't need Stella Jr. if you got into shape and dieted.

JACOB: Yeah yeah yeah. Like I said, one issue at a time. Small steps. Learn to crawl et cetera, et cetera, et cetera.

DESTINY: Why is it so hard to do the smart thing? You obviously know your life's in rough shape. So shape up!

The Rick Astley song plays on the computer.

DESTINY: Oh my god, Rick!

She runs to her computer.

JACOB: I thought you were over—

DESTINY: Shut up!

She puts the headphones on and listens. It's the worst news possible. She slowly puts the headphones down.

JACOB: Not good news?

DESTINY: Actually, it's great news. For him. He's getting married. Yippee. I'm so happy for him.

Paula Jean Prudat (Destiny)

JACOB: To the actress?

DESTINY: Yes, to the fucking actress!

She closes the laptop lid then pounds the shit out of it.

Fuck fuck fuck fuck fuck fucking fuck!

She throws it to the floor and stomps on it.

Fucking fucking fuck fuck fuck fuck!

The assault continues. JACOB clutches Stella Jr. to his chest.

Fuck fuck fuck fuck fuck fuck fuck fuck!

She suddenly stops. Pause. Deep breaths. She lights up a smoke. Pause.

I think I just had an orgasm.

She looks at JACOB. Something in her eyes scares the shit out of him. He drops the defibrillator and runs for his life. She takes a long inhale on the smoke. Pause.

Black out.

Scene 4

ISAAC sits alone in the principal's office of the residential school. No furniture. It's dusty. It faces east, so the sun shines in brightly through the windows. ISAAC has some slides that he looks at with the sunlight. Some old school boxes remain. JACOB enters, haggard.

ISAAC: What happened to you?

JACOB: I think I'm in love. I mean, really in love. She's the woman of my dreams. She's something else, Ike.

ISAAC: You look terrible.

JACOB: I'm a little winded, yeah.

ISAAC: Did you two just have sex or something?

JACOB: It was something alright. Wow! She's dangerous. I just need to catch my breath for a minute.

ISAAC: Have a seat.

JACOB: This is the principal's office? You can tell. It still has that aura of power and fear. Mostly fear.

He opens a box and looks through it.

What are you doing here, Isaac?

ISAAC: Going through my portfolio. The light's best here.

JACOB: I mean, what are you doing here? On the reserve?

ISAAC: I wanted to do some good.

JACOB: For who? Yourself?

ISAAC: For the people here. Our people.

JACOB: "Our people?" You say that like you own them or something.

ISAAC: I belong to them. We both do.

JACOB: Really? You really feel that way?

ISAAC: Yes.

JACOB: Then why did you move into the residential school?

ISAAC: I didn't want to take a house away from another family.

JACOB: Come on, Isaac. You've been away for twenty-five years and then you picked the one place everyone stays away from. This isn't reaching out to "our people." This is, "I'm back, leave me the fuck alone!"

ISAAC: Why are you back?

JACOB: To cover a graduation.

ISAAC: I don't believe you.

JACOB: Hey, phone my former assignment editor if you want.

ISAAC: Former?

JACOB: I got fired. I think.

ISAAC: Because you missed the graduation?

JACOB: That. And I'm just tired of filing bullshit stories.

ISAAC: So you quit.

JACOB: Yeah. Must run in the family.

ISAAC: What do you mean by that?

JACOB: You're quitting.

ISAAC: They don't need me here. I was set up. A patsy.

JACOB: So you're just going to leave?

ISAAC: I can't do anything for this place. It's either the government or the people themselves who won't move. It's like they're in a dance together for mutual misery. I want to do something that means...something...something real.

JACOB: So you want to go back to where you're comfortable. It's like me going back to the booze. War is a place for you to hide. You need to find a place more miserable than here to feel good about yourself.

ISAAC: War makes sense. Even the chaos makes sense.

JACOB: Are you telling me running a reserve is harder than working in a war zone? That's the funniest thing I've ever heard.

ISAAC: Nothing about running a reserve makes sense. And now I find out I got set up by Chief Charlie to take the fall. He knew this was about happen. But I'll look like the bad guy when the shit hits the fan. Fine. I won't be here. I'm sure I can get a gig in Afghanistan or Iraq.

JACOB: Don't you guys have a support group of some kind? A War Junkies Anonymous?

ISAAC: I'm not wanted here. No point sticking around.

JACOB: No. You're realizing that the problems here are more complicated than you'd like—that simplistic solutions don't work. Just like the problems you're having.

ISAAC: Fuck you, Jacob!

JACOB: You know I'm right.

ISAAC: I'm returning to photojournalism. It's still a noble thing to do.

JACOB: But I thought you were sick of that.

ISAAC: This is where I was successful—where I made a difference—where I need to go.

JACOB: But you're not the same man who took these. Look at them—they're horrific. You want to be this man again?

ISAAC: I was a man who cared about the suffering of others. Who made sure people saw and remembered these things.

JACOB: Yeah, but why do you have to do it? There are lots of journalists willing to get near the shit and tell that story.

ISAAC: Their eyes, Jake. *(He shows the slides to JACOB.)* Look into their eyes and tell me they're not important—that their stories are irrelevant. Fear. Anguish. Panic. But something else. Even when they're seconds away from death there's a spark—they're fighting for their lives until the very end. They've endured so much and yet they keep fighting. That's what I see when I'm there. But here. In a land so rich, I see so much helplessness.

JACOB: Holy crap! What are you like at parties? "Oh great, here comes Major Bringdown."

ISAAC: I'm serious.

JACOB: So am I. Look at yourself. You've experience some of the worst humanity can dish out and yet you're still a decent human being. No one can walk through that much misery and not get scarred but you still keep trying to do good. You can be full of yourself once in a while but you have a life worth celebrating—not always wallowing in sadness. But you're running away.

ISAAC: I'm not running.

JACOB: That's why you're in the tallest tower in the castle waiting for your Princess Charming to rescue you. You're living a fairy tale, friend. You're still chief for two and half more years. Use it! Fight for something good here. Show some of that spark you see in these people's eyes. And get rid of this goddamned building.

ISAAC: I want to keep it as a memorial to the survivors of the residential schools.

JACOB: Yeah yeah yeah. A monument to sadness.

ISAAC: We need to remember what happened here and why it happened.

JACOB: No, we need to remember that we won. The

government and the churches came and tried to eliminate us—but they didn't. We're still here. They picked on us as kids. As kids! At our weakest and most vulnerable and we still endured. We didn't lose our spirit—our spark—our will to fight. If we did then we wouldn't be here having this conversation. So if you want a monument to residential schools, make it a giant middle finger with "NICE TRY, FUCKERS!" engraved on the bottom! And we have a big victory dance here every year. Tell the fuckers we forgive them and honour the survivors like veterans.

JACOB does an impromptu round dance but with his middle fingers raised.

ISAAC: Now you're talking about simplistic solutions.

JACOB: Oh, you think forgiveness is simple? Tells me you haven't tried it yet.

ISAAC: Who am I supposed to forgive? My life is fine.

JACOB: You're not fine. You're still mourning Zia. And she's been dead for ten years.

ISAAC: It was because of her I came back. Every day I'm here, I ask myself, what the fuck am I doing? I never wanted to see this place again. As she was dying, she kept saying I had to come back. So I did. Because I loved her and wanted to honour her memory. But if it wasn't for the cancer... I can't help it, Jacob...being here just makes me pissed off she died on me. It makes no sense. But that's how I feel. I resent her for abandoning me. And then I get pissed off at myself for being pissed off at her.

JACOB: Have you ever forgiven her for dying?

ISAAC: That makes no sense. She didn't get cancer to piss me off.

JACOB: You feel angry at her. It's there. Whatever's really

eating at your soul is hidden in that. You're just putting her face on it right now.

ISAAC: It's that easy?

JACOB: Fuck no. True forgiveness has to be unconditional. It's going to put you through the wringer. Why do you think I still need to drink? But take your time. And don't kill yourself for feeling what you feel. It's only human. Just stop running away.

ISAAC: I have nothing here, Jake. No reason to stay.

JACOB sucker punches ISAAC.

ISAAC: *(Holding his jaw.)* Fuck Jacob! What the fuck!

He tries to punch ISAAC again. ISAAC blocks it. They fight. But they're uncoordinated and pathetic. DESTINY enters.

DESTINY: What the fuck, guys!

They stop.

ISAAC: He attacked me.

DESTINY: Jacob?

JACOB exits to one of the other rooms. DESTINY looks at ISAAC's jaw.

Does it hurt?

ISAAC: No. He punches like a girl.

DESTINY: Oh really. Care to compare?

She makes a fist.

ISAAC: I'm just saying…nothing.

DESTINY: What happened?

ISAAC: I'm thinking of going back to photojournalism.

DESTINY: Wow. That's it. You're just going to abandon these people here. And Jake.

ISAAC: Jake can handle himself.

DESTINY: You are so cold. No wonder you could work in war zones, you have no feelings for anyone!

ISAAC: Hang on a minute!

DESTINY: He's your only family!

She punches him.

ISAAC: Ow! What the hell!

DESTINY: You feel something now?

ISAAC: Pissed off!

DESTINY: Yeah. Why?

ISAAC: Because you're hitting me for no reason!

She punches him again.

Fuck!

DESTINY: Reasons? You need reasons? How about you're a fucking retard!

ISAAC: I didn't do anything!

DESTINY: You're rejecting him! He has no one else except you! Ever thought of that? For a smart guy, you can be an idiot.

ISAAC: Why do you care?

DESTINY: Because... I want to work with you and you're acting stupid and this is not how I thought this would happen.

ISAAC: What would happen?

DESTINY: Open your eyes!

Pause. He doesn't get it. She grabs him. He thinks he's about to get punched and flinches but she kisses him passionately then she pushes him away.

DESTINY: That's the last one. Unless you smarten the fuck up.

ISAAC: I just thought you were drunk. That other time.

DESTINY: Well now you know, you big dummy.

JACOB storms by, carrying his bags and cleansing drink. He's headed for the door. ISAAC cuts him off.

ISAAC: Jacob.

JACOB: I don't want to hurt you. Get out of my way.

ISAAC: I'm sorry.

JACOB: Fuck off!

ISAAC: Jacob, wait! Don't go. *(Pause.)* Jake, look at me. Please look at me. Look at me! *(Pause.)* I'm sorry. I am so fucking sorry. For running away. For staying away so long. For all that time when I should've… Forgive me. Please forgive me. Please…I don't want to be alone. You're all the family I got.

JACOB thinks about it then grabs ISAAC in a strong bear hug.

JACOB: Ike?

ISAAC: Yeah?

JACOB: I wanted to be you. I wanted the old man to love me like he loved you. I was never good enough. I was never good enough. I was never good enough! I was never good enough!

Pause.

ISAAC: Jacob.

JACOB: Yeah, cuz?

ISAAC: Can't breathe!

JACOB lets go.

JACOB: Sorry.

ISAAC: It's going to take me awhile to get used to this.

JACOB: Take all the time you need. I'm not going anywhere?

ISAAC: You're not? You're staying here?

JACOB: *(Simultaneously with ISAAC.)* Well, no, I mean, I'm not leaving the country or anything. I'm sure I can find— Well, I don't want to impose. Really?

ISAAC: *(Simultaneously with JACOB.)* But if you want to, you can stay. As long as you want. Honest, I want you to stay. Yes! Really! I insist. Put your bags away.

JACOB: Cool.

JACOB exits with his stuff.

ISAAC: What if he never leaves?

DESTINY: Tell him to leave when you want him to leave.

ISAAC: Should I tell him now?

DESTINY: Give it a little time. Jeez. You're going to take some work, aren't you.

ISAAC: So you're sticking around too?

DESTINY: As long as we're partners. I mean, in getting the reserve out of debt. Not partners in the other— not yet, anyway— I'm not promising— but let's just— oh geez.

ISAAC: OK, OK. I think I understand. We just—

DESTINY: We?

ISAAC: One step at a time. Alright?

DESTINY: One step at a time.

ISAAC: And Rick?

DESTINY: I wish him well.

ISAAC: You shouldn't scowl when you say that.

DESTINY: Give me time. Are you going to keep living in the old school? *(In ZIA's accent.)* There's so much pain here, so much anger.

ISAAC: At least they acknowledge it… Wait? What did you say?

DESTINY: I said, it's a depressing place. You shouldn't live here anymore.

ISAAC stares at her. pause.

What?

ISAAC: You just gave me a great idea.

JACOB returns wearing only his underwear a la Act I Scene 5.

(Simultaneously with JACOB.) Really? Five seconds and you're already in your gotch? Are you going to walk around like that all the time? Destiny is right here! Are you going to be like this when we have visitors? Put a robe on or something.

JACOB: *(Simultaneously with ISAAC.)* What? I'm just trying to be comfortable. This is how I relax. Hey look, if this is too real for you. She's already seen me like this. Visitors? Who's going to visit us here?

DESTINY: Hey! Guys! Knock it off.

ISAAC: Jacob, now that you're going to be around for a while, I want you to do something.

JACOB: OK, I know I just moved in and everything, but you don't have to get bossy so quickly.

ISAAC: Oh sorry, am I interfering with your plans?

JACOB: I'll look for another job, if that's what you're asking.

ISAAC: No, I'm not asking that.

JACOB: Because I've always pulled my own weight. I'm not some sponge!

ISAAC: I didn't say you were. Look. Just let me finish before you get all bent out of shape. Can you do that?

JACOB: OK. What's on your mind?

ISAAC: Are you done with APTN?

JACOB: More than likely.

ISAAC: Do you want to work with me on a project?

JACOB: You're hiring your only cousin to work for the band? That wouldn't look too good, chief.

DESTINY: I gotta say I agree.

ISAAC: Not for the band, for me. I'll be paying you, not Thunder Cree.

JACOB: Paying me how much? I don't want to get exploited. Honest wages for honest work.

ISAAC: Exploited? I wouldn't exploit you!

JACOB: I'm not some cheap running shoe you can buy at Giant Tiger.

ISAAC: What are you talking about?

JACOB: Just protecting my rights. And dignity.

ISAAC: OK, whatever they paid you at APTN. Is that dignified enough?

JACOB: I agree to your terms. What's the project?

ISAAC: You guys are both right. This building must be torn down. And when it is, Jake and I will document it. With video and photos, and interviews with the former students. I'll fund it. This will be Zia's legacy. And then we'll take it across Canada as a multi-media memorial. We may not have the building but we'll have the stories. We'll make Canada and the rest of the world look into their eyes and hear the stories of the survivors—no, the veterans, to honour the children who became warriors because they were sent to this place. No one is going to forget what happened here. But we'll also show them that we are still here. That our spirit may have been attacked but it was never taken. We still have it. And we will never lose it.

Historic photos of residential schools and survivors are beamed over the entire set and hold until the end of the play..

THE VOICES OF FORMER STUDENTS: "The last memory of my mother was her walking away from me when she left me at the school." "Our Father, who art in heaven, hallowed be Thy name." "I had fun here, we played a lot of sports." "The principal cut my braids off." "The food was awful, it was always awful." "The nuns would beat me if I spoke Cree." "At night, I tried not to cry."

"I could see my parents' house from the top floor of the school." "I ran away as much as I could. Even after the teachers whipped me, I'd run away again."... *(The voices fade.)*

Black out.

The End.